D1064735

EDGE
BOOKS

VS

BUG WARS

ASSASSIN
BUG VS. OGRE-FACED
SPIDER

BY ALICIA Z. KLEPEIS

WHEN CUNNING
HUNTERS COLLIDE

CONSULTANT:
Christiane Weirauch
Professor of Entomology,
Department of Entomology
University of California, Riverside

CAPSTONE PRESS
a capstone imprint

Edge Books are published by Capstone Press,
1710 Roe Crest Drive, North Mankato, Minnesota 56003
www.mycapstone.com

Library of Congress Cataloging-in-Publication Data
Klepeis, Alicia, 1971–author.
Assassin bug vs. Ogre-faced spider : when cunning hunters collide / by Alicia Klepeis.
pages cm.—(Edge books. Bug wars)
Audience: Ages 9–10.
Audience: Grades 4 to 6.
Summary: "Describes the characteristics of assassin bugs and ogre-faced spiders, and what
may happen when these bugs encounter one another in nature"—Provided by publisher.
ISBN 978-1-4914-8065-6 (library binding)
ISBN 978-1-4914-8069-4 (paperback)
ISBN 978-1-4914-8073-1 (eBook PDF)
1. Assassin bugs—Juvenile literature. 2. Deinopis—Juvenile literature. 3. Spiders—Juvenile
literature. 4. Predatory animals—Juvenile literature. I. Title. II. Title: Assassin bug versus
Ogre-faced spider.
QL523.R4K54 2016
595—dc23   2015024333

Editorial Credits
Aaron Sautter, editor; Russell Griesmer, designer; Jo Miller, media researcher;
Katy LaVigne, production specialist

Photo Credits
Alamy: Daniel Borzynski, 15, Steve Bloom Images, 27, (top); Minden Pictures: Kazuo
Unno, Nature Production, 23; Newscom: Arco Images G/picture alliance/Huetter, C.,
25, Minden Pictures/Ch"len Lee, 24, Minden Pictures/Stephen Dalton, 19, Photoshot/
NHPA/Gerhard Koertner, 29, Photoshot/NHPA/Nick Garbutt, 17; Science Source: ANT
Photo Library, 21, John Serrao, 11, Shutterstock: Melinda Fawver, Cover (left), 5, 7, 9, 22,
Paul Looyen, Cover (right), 7, Peter Waters, 4, Robyn Butler, 6, Tom Grundy, 27, (bottom);
SuperStock: NaturePL, 13

Design Elements
Capstone and Shutterstock

Printed and bound in US.
007521CGS16

TABLE OF CONTENTS

WELCOME TO BUG WARS!

Some bugs are ferocious hunters. They search for **prey**, kill it, and eat it. These fierce **predators** often have clear advantages over other bugs. But in Bug Wars, that's not the case. These flesh-eating bugs are all equipped with fangs, **venom**, sticky webs, and other deadly weapons. In Bug Wars you never know which hunter will end up victorious!

prey—an animal hunted by another animal for food
predator—an animal that hunts other animals for food
venom—poisonous liquid produced by some animals

DEADLY HUNTERS

You're about to watch an Assassin Bug and an Ogre-Faced Spider in a fight to the death. But first you'll learn how these killer bugs match up against each other. You'll discover their deadly weapons and how they fight in combat. Finally, you'll get to watch from a front row seat as they duke it out!

THE COMBATANTS

Assassin bugs and ogre-faced spiders may not encounter each other often in the wild. But they do share some territory. Both live in warm climates in North and South America, Africa, Asia, and Australia.

Although these predators thrive in warm temperatures, they are found in a variety of **habitats**. Assassin bugs live in grasslands, forests, and even deserts. Meanwhile, ogre-faced spiders are often found in **bushlands** and tropical forests.

Both of these hunters can destroy other bugs easily. An assassin bug's bite can **paralyze** a cockroach in just 4 seconds! And the ogre-faced spider eats all sorts of insects from beetles to butterflies.

Assassin bugs and ogre-faced spiders don't always battle each other. They usually munch on smaller insects. But you never know—when these bugs are hungry, they'll take food wherever they can find it!

FIERCE FACT

THERE ARE NEARLY 7,000 SPECIES OF ASSASSIN BUGS IN THE WORLD.

habitat—the natural place and conditions in which a plant or animal lives

bushland—a somewhat dry area of land where trees and shrubs grow

paralyze—to cause a loss of the ability to control the muscles

SIZE AND SPEED

The wheel bug is one of the world's largest assassin bugs. It can measure up to 1.5 inches (3.8 centimeters) long, or about the size of a large paperclip. Assassin bugs move slowly. They walk with a bouncy step at about 0.4 to 1.2 inches (1 to 3 cm) per second. They are also slow and clumsy fliers. But the slow walking speed of these bugs can be deceiving. These hunters can move especially fast when striking at prey. An assassin bug's strike happens in less than 0.1 second. That's faster than people can blink their eyes!

The ogre-faced spider is larger than an assassin bug. Including its legs, this scary spider can be up to 3 inches (7.6 cm) long. The ogre-faced spider is also much faster than an assassin bug. With its long legs, the spider can run up to 4 inches (10 cm) per second.

The highlight of the spider's speed is seen when catching its prey. This hunter can strike in just one thousandth of a second. That's 10 times faster than a lightning bolt! The spider's speed is a huge advantage when catching prey—and during a fight.

RATING 2

ASSASSIN BUG:
slow mover,
fast striker

RATING 4

**OGRE-FACED
SPIDER:**
fast mover,
super-fast striker

FIERCE FACT

THE SCIENTIFIC NAME FOR OGRE-FACED SPIDERS IS
DEINOPIS, WHICH MEANS "TERRIBLE APPEARANCE."
SOME PEOPLE THINK THESE SPIDERS' HUGE EYES
MAKE THEM LOOK LIKE OGRES.

ASSASSIN BUG DEFENSES

Like most insects, the assassin bug has an **exoskeleton**. This hard armorlike covering helps protect it during an attack. The wheel bug's jagged body armor is especially sturdy. The teethlike projections on the bug's back may make it difficult for a predator to eat it.

Besides being hard and tough, an assassin bug's exoskeleton serves another purpose. Its color enables the bug to either warn or hide from enemies. Some assassin bugs have bright colors to warn predators that the bugs are dangerous. Other assassin bugs have gray, black, or brown bodies. These colors provide excellent **camouflage**. The bugs often blend in easily with plants. This helps them stay hidden from both predators and prey.

exoskeleton—a structure on the outside of an animal that gives it support
camouflage—coloring or covering that makes animals, people, and objects look like their surroundings

ASSASSIN BUG:
tough exoskeleton,
great camouflage

FIERCE FACT

IF DISTURBED, SOME ASSASSIN BUGS
CAN SPRAY A STINGING MIST THAT
CHASES AWAY PREDATORS.

OGRE-FACED SPIDER DEFENSES

The ogre-faced spider has camouflage of its own. Its brown coloring and long slender legs make it look like a stick. This makes the spider tough for other bugs to spot. This is especially true when it lies stretched out on a branch.

The ogre-faced spider's best defense is its excellent vision. Its two huge eyes give it better night vision than cats or even owls! Its great vision gives the spider a huge advantage over its enemies.

Ogre-faced spiders have one other incredible defense. If a leg becomes caught or damaged, these spiders can shed the injured limb and keep moving. Special body parts inside the spider then work to reduce any bleeding. This process is called **autotomy**, and it can be very useful in a fight.

autotomy—the ability of some animals to safely shed a damaged or trapped body part

RATING

3

OGRE-FACED SPIDER:
excellent vision,
good camouflage

ASSASSIN BUG WEAPONS

The assassin bug is a killing machine. It has many dangerous weapons to use when hunting and fighting. Many of these bugs can extend their front legs outward to grasp prey. Some assassin bugs have spines on these legs that help them hold onto victims.

The assassin bug's mouthparts are similar to a mosquito's. They are specialized for stabbing and sucking. Some insects use their **mandibles** for chomping. But the assassin bug's mandibles form part of its strawlike **rostrum**. The rostrum is strong and beaklike. It can stab right through its prey's exoskeleton.

The assassin bug's rostrum is dangerous. But its deadliest weapon is its venom. The venom can paralyze prey within seconds and liquefy its insides.

mandibles—strong mouthparts used for chewing
rostrum—a strong, piercing mouthpart used by some insects for hunting prey

RATING ▮▮▮▮▯▯ **3**

ASSASSIN BUG:
sharp rostrum,
deadly venom

FIERCE FACT

WHEN NOT IN USE, THE ASSASSIN BUG CAN
TUCK ITS ROSTRUM NEATLY INTO A NARROW
GROOVE BETWEEN ITS FRONT LEGS.

OGRE-FACED SPIDER WEAPONS

The ogre-faced spider is one scary-looking predator. Its two long fangs can easily pierce an enemy's flesh. The fangs are also important tools for injecting the spider's venom into its prey. The venom paralyzes prey very quickly. Victims are usually unable to move when the spider begins munching on them!

The spider's venom is nasty stuff. But this crafty hunter uses another impressive weapon. It makes a postage-stamp sized web that spreads out like a net. The web is made of special **cribellum silk**. This fuzzy silk snags and sticks to insects' legs. The spider uses its special net to trap its prey with lightning speed.

cribellum silk—a type of spider silk made of tiny fibers that has a woolly appearance; insects easily get tangled and caught in this type of silk

RATING

◻◻◻◻◻ 4

OGRE-FACED SPIDER:
wicked web

FIERCE FACT

IF THE OGRE-FACED SPIDER DOESN'T USE ITS WEB DURING THE NIGHT, IT WILL EAT IT. THE SPIDER THEN MAKES A NEW NET THE NEXT NIGHT.

ASSASSIN BUG ATTACK STYLE

The assassin bug is a creepy hunter. It uses its antennae to sense vibrations. Once prey is found, the bug carefully sneaks up on it. The hunter moves in a bouncy and irregular way. Once the assassin bug is close enough, it strikes viciously. The predator plunges its sharp rostrum repeatedly into the prey's body.

But stabbing its prey is only part of the assassin bug's attack. It also squirts venom into its victim's body. The assassin bug's powerful venom starts to act in just 3 to 5 seconds. Within 15 seconds the prey can't move and its insides quickly turn to liquid. The assassin bug then sucks out the soupy guts before moving on to find its next victim.

3

ASSASSIN BUG:
sharp rostrum,
deadly venom

FIERCE
FACT

THE ASSASSIN BUG'S SALIVA WORKS AS AN ANESTHETIC.
IN MOST CASES ITS PREY DOESN'T FEEL PAIN.

anesthetic—a substance that reduces sensitivity to pain

OGRE-FACED SPIDER ATTACK STYLE

The ogre-faced spider is a patient hunter. Its camouflaged body helps keep it hidden from prey. The spider holds its woven net in its four front legs. Its head dangles down as it waits for prey to pass by. The spider's body has tiny hairs that can sense when insects are moving nearby.

The ogre-faced spider stays perfectly still as it waits. When prey touches one of the net's anchoring threads, the spider knows its next meal is within reach. Faster than lightning, the ogre-faced spider casts its net over its victim. The net quickly contracts and tangles the unlucky bug in its sticky threads. The spider then injects venom into its victim with its sharp fangs. Lightning-quick reflexes and web wrapping skills make the ogre-faced spider a fearsome predator.

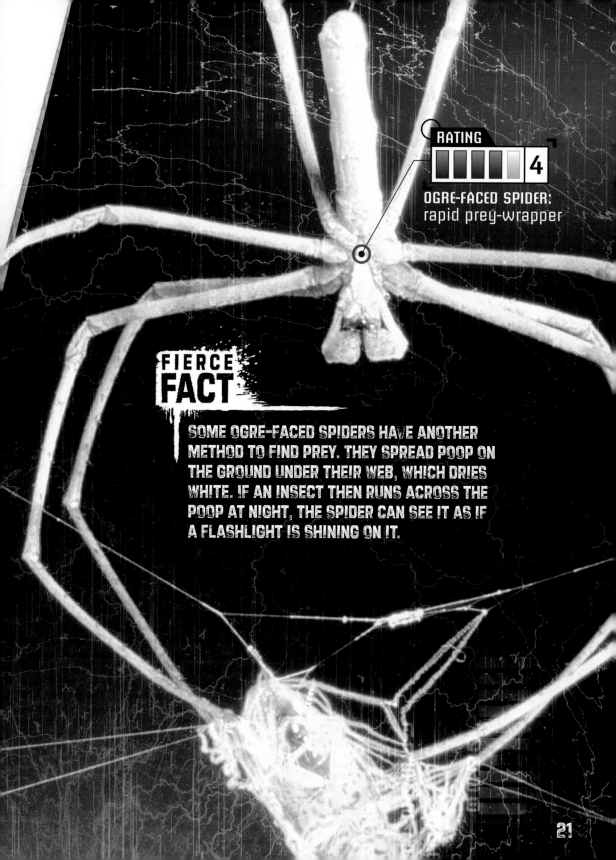

FIERCE FACT

SOME OGRE-FACED SPIDERS HAVE ANOTHER METHOD TO FIND PREY. THEY SPREAD POOP ON THE GROUND UNDER THEIR WEB, WHICH DRIES WHITE. IF AN INSECT THEN RUNS ACROSS THE POOP AT NIGHT, THE SPIDER CAN SEE IT AS IF A FLASHLIGHT IS SHINING ON IT.

Are you prepared for a ferocious fight? These two hungry flesh-eating bugs are looking for their next meal. But they're about to collide in a fierce battle. In one corner is the gut-piercing assassin bug! It's sneaky and packs a secret hidden weapon. In the other corner is its fearsome foe—the ogre-faced spider! Even its name sounds frightening. It's a lightning-quick killer. Nobody knows which of these bugs will win. But one thing is certain—these fearsome hunters will keep battling until the bitter end.

You've got a front row seat. So grab your favorite snack, turn the page, and get ready to enjoy the battle!

ONE LAST THING...

This fight is made up, just like in your favorite movies. These two bugs may occasionally fight each other in nature, but it's hard to say who would win. However, we know these bugs are ferocious fighters. So if you like a good bug battle, this should be a great show!

GUTS AND GLORY

It's nighttime in the forest. An ogre-faced spider has found a perfect spot to hide. His sticklike body blends in perfectly with the nearby branches. He's nearly invisible to other creatures. He hangs upside down and scans the area with his huge, bulging eyes. Between his front legs he holds his trap, a bluish-white web of special silk.

Nearby an assassin bug is also on the prowl. He's hungry and hopes to find a tasty meal. His antennae twitch, sensing the movement of other bugs creeping below him. Soon he sees a spider web gleaming in the faint moonlight. He unpacks his deadly rostrum from its tucked-away position. He's ready for action.

The ogre-faced spider's bulging eyeballs peer into the darkness. Finally, it spots the smaller assassin bug. The spider tracks his prey, patiently but with purpose. He is waiting for it to come closer—so that he can strike!

But the assassin bug has its own plans. He hopes to turn the spider into a midnight meal. The assassin bug tries plucking on the spider's web. Bad choice! He touched one of the web's "trip wires." The spider quickly swoops down to attack the assassin bug.

FIERCE FACT

THREAD-LEGGED BUGS SOMETIMES LURE SPIDERS BY PLUCKING THE THREADS OF THEIR WEBS. THIS DRAWS THE SPIDERS CLOSER, ALLOWING THE THREAD-LEGGED BUGS TO STRIKE.

But the assassin bug fights back. The two hunters tussle. Each lashes out at the other with all its might. The assassin bug tries to jab the ogre-faced spider with his beaklike rostrum, but misses. During the deadly duel, one of the spider's legs is torn off! The ogre-faced spider staggers back, reeling from his nasty injury. The bleeding quickly stops, thanks to the spider's internal shutoff valve. He'll grow a new leg later. Right now, it's time to get back into the fight.

For a moment it looks like the assassin bug has the advantage. But then he makes a fatal mistake. He wanders underneath his spider foe. In a flash, the ogre-faced spider casts his special web over his prey. The assassin bug is trapped. He tries once more to stab the spider with his rostrum. But the ogre-faced spider acts fast to avoid being speared by his foe. Keeping the assassin bug as far away as possible, the cunning spider quickly wraps his prey in layers of sticky silk.

FIERCE FACT

SOME TYPES OF SPIDER SILK ARE STRONGER THAN STEEL.

Before long the assassin bug is bound tightly like a mummy. He can do nothing. Knowing his prey can't move, the ogre-faced spider injects his victim with paralyzing venom. The assassin bug is powerless. He can't use his legs or rostrum anymore. He has lost the battle. Death comes swiftly for the assassin bug. Soon the ogre-faced spider will be slurping up the dissolved innards of his prey. He'll be eating well tonight!

GLOSSARY

anesthetic (an-iss-THET-ik)—a substance that reduces sensitivity to pain

autotomy (uh-TAH-tuh-mee)—the ability of some animals to safely shed a damaged or trapped body part

bushland (BUSH-land)—a somewhat dry area of land where trees and shrubs grow

camouflage (KA-muh-flahzh)—coloring or covering that makes animals, people, and objects look like their surroundings

cribellum silk (krih-BEL-uhm SILK)—a type of spider silk made of tiny fibers that has a woolly appearance; insects easily get tangled and caught in this type of silk

exoskeleton (ek-soh-SKE-luh-tuhn)—a structure on the outside of an animal that gives it support

habitat (HAB-uh-tat)—the natural place and conditions in which a plant or animal lives

mandibles (MAN-duh-buhlz)—strong mouthparts used for chewing

paralyze (PAYR-uh-lize)—to cause a loss of the ability to control the muscles

predator (PRED-uh-tur)—an animal that hunts other animals for food

prey (PRAY)—an animal hunted by another animal for food

rostrum (RAW-struhm)—a strong, piercing mouthpart used by some insects for hunting prey

venom (VEN-uhm)—poisonous liquid produced by some animals

READ MORE

Bingham, Caroline. *Everything You Need To Know About Bugs.* New York: DK Publishing, 2015.

Gleason, Carrie. *Everything Insects: All the Facts, Photos, and Fun to Make You Buzz!* Washington, D.C.: National Geographic, 2015.

Parker, Steve. *Bug Wars: Deadly Insects And Spiders Go Head-To-Head.* New York: Ticktock Books, 2014.

INTERNET SITES

FactHound offers a safe, fun way to find Internet sites related to this book. All of the sites on FactHound have been researched by our staff.

Here's all you do:

Visit *www.facthound.com*

Type in this code: 9781491480656

Check out projects, games and lots more at
www.capstonekids.com

INDEX